Dedicated to
Aindriú, Alannah, Aviyah, Violet, Naomi, Leora
Michael, Holly, Rhyna and Lilou

ABOUT THE AUTHOR

After a career as a designer and illustrator, Don Conroy went on to become a household name through his appearances on RTE's long-running television series, *The Den*. He is also the author of numerous children's books, and is actively involved in wildlife conservation.

Over the years Don's passion for teaching art has continued. He has held many workshops for young people at Dublin Zoo, the National Gallery, the Natural History Museum, and in libraries, schools and festivals throughout the country.

DRAW with DON

DON CONROY

MENTOR BOOKS

Published in 2016 by:
Mentor Books Ltd.
43 Furze Road
Sandyford Industrial Estate
Dublin 18
Republic of Ireland
Tel: +353 1 295 2112/3
Fax: +353 1 295 2114
e-mail: admin@mentorbooks.ie
www.mentorbooks.ie

ISBN: 978-1-909417-47-2

Editing, design and layout: Nicola Sedgwick
Cover design: Kathryn O'Sullivan

Printed in the EU

ACKNOWLEDGEMENTS

Thanks to all my family,
especially to Gay and Sarah
for their invaluable help.
Thanks also to my editors,
in particular to Nicola,
and the staff at Mentor Books.

CONTENTS

Introduction 7

Getting Started 9
   Materials Needed 9
   Simple Basic Heads 9
   Character Height 11
   Head Shapes 12
   Fitting Heads to Bodies 15
   Making Characters
    Younger and Older 16
   Oval Head Development 17
   Three-Quarter Angle 18
   More Head Angles 19
   Witch Business for Halloween 21
   Eyes, Noses and Mouths 22
   Creating Characters' Expressions . . 24
   Sinister Characters 25
   Realistic and Cartoon Hands 26
   From Realistic to Cartoon Hands . . 27
   Various Hands! 28
   Moving Your Character 29
   From Action Figure
    to Egyptian Mummy 31
   From Action Figure
    to Quizzical Wizard 32

Spooks and Spirits 33
   Ghostly Scream 34
   Doubly Scary 35
   Old Lady Spirit 36

GALLERY - Unexpected Visitors 37
   Young Lady Spirit 38
   Ghost Gallery 39
   High Spirits 40

Witches 41
   Let's Draw Witches! 42
   Abbiewail and the New Broom 42
   The Many Faces of Abbiewail 44
   Glamorous Scarea 45
   Grimly in a Tizzy. 46
   Creating a Witch's Face 48
   Various Witches' Faces
   and Expressions 49

Vampires 51
   Welcome to the World
    of Vampires 52
   Dracula Awakens 52
   Nosferatu the Undead 55

GALLERY - Count and
Countess Dracula 56
   Various Vampires 57
   More Vampires to Get your Teeth into . 58
   Early Screen Vampire 59
   Vampire Ladies 60

Grave Robbers 61
   Grave Concern 62
   Victorian Grave Robber 64

GALLERY - Bony Fiddler 66

Werewolves and Zombies 67
   Zombies on the Prowl 68
   Werewolves on the Howl 70

Creepy Humans 71
   Mr Hyde 72
   Sinister Butler 73

Spooky Faces 75
   The Scared, the Bad and the Ugly . . 76

Fantastic Creatures 79
   Hairy Monster on the Run 80
   A Monster Selection 81
   Night Mare 82
   Grumpy Bigfoot 83

GALLERY - A Big Monster Hello . 84

Giants and Ogres 85
   Gentle Giant 86
   Obnoxious Ogres 88

From Books and Legends 89
   Headless Man
   and Marley's Ghost 90
   Jinn and Genie 91
   Menacing Mummys 92

Wizards and Sorcerers 93
   Wise Wizard and Sly Sorcerers . . . 94

INTRODUCTION

Monsters come in all shapes and forms (some even formless). Scary creatures such as vampires, werewolves, ghouls, zombies, giants, ogres, witches to name just a few, have inhabited our ancient cultures in the form of myths, legends and in our folklore. Literature and popular culture have given us scary creatures like Mary Shelley's Frankenstein and Bram Stoker's Count Dracula.

These popular tales have spawned countless more eerie tales to satisfy the modern audience through novels, graphic and cartoon comics, and magazines. Television and cinema fill our screens with scary shows such as Supernatural, Buffy the Vampire Slayer, and a host of other shows. It seems people of all ages enjoy an ol' scare, whether on screen or between the safety of two covers of a novel. I admit I too enjoy a good spooky book or TV show or film as long as it's not too gory.

Here between these two covers you will find lots of monsters to tackle – but I don't mean literally! Armed not with a sword, crucifix, stake or garlic to take on these creatures, instead you have paper and pencil. You will also be given plenty of tips throughout the book on how to draw your own cartoon monsters!

The result is not so much to scare as to give one a laugh or two. The main thing is to have fun and enjoy.

Warmest regards

Don Conroy

GETTING STARTED

Materials Needed

- Sketchpad or cartridge paper
- HB and 2B pencils
- Watercolour set
- Pen, brush and Indian ink
- Felt-tipped marker
- Eraser

Simple Basic Heads

Let's begin with circles as shown. Imagine a head as a globe, and draw a cross in the middle of the circle to help you position the facial features. The vertical line shows the middle of the face and the horizontal is the eye guideline. The eyes go above the nose and the mouth goes below the ears on either side of circle. By turning the globe the vertical should move to position as shown at bottom of column 2. This helps you draw a two-third view. Now with paper and a pencil have a go copying these basic faces.

COLUMN 1   **COLUMN 2**

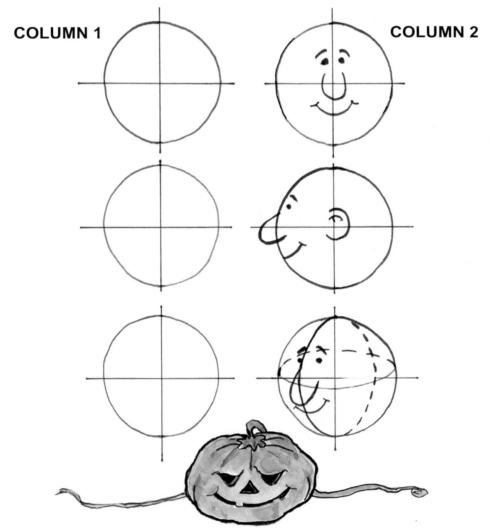

MONSTERS GALORE!

Here are more examples of the basic head.
1. Head on view
2. Side view, looking right
3. Side view, looking left
4 Two-third view, looking right or left using dotted line
5. Looking up
6. Looking down

Remember to think of a globe when drawing a simple head.

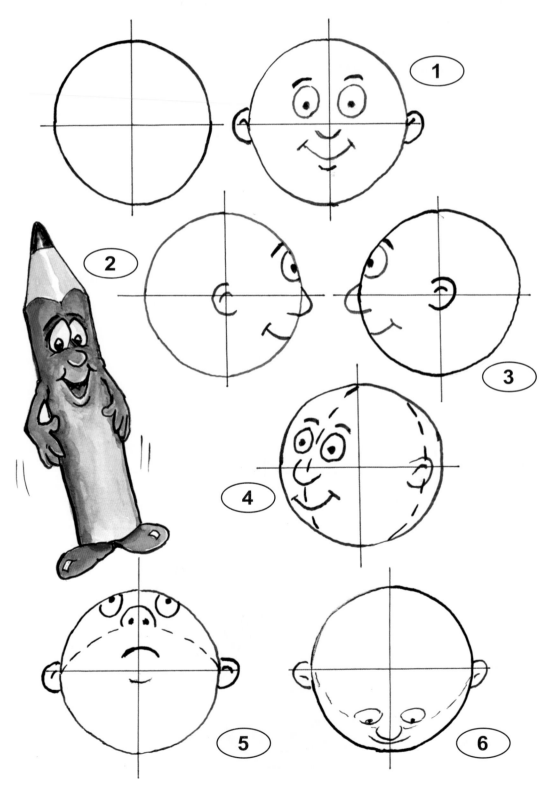

Character Height

When drawing a realistic adult figure, the body can be measured as six to seven heads high.

However, when we approach drawing graphic novel figures or cartoon characters the measurements change. When drawing superheroes the artist usually draws the figure about eight to nine heads high, and as seen below with the little wizard, cartoon characters are drawn only about three to four heads high.

Head Shapes

Differently-shaped heads make interesting characters!

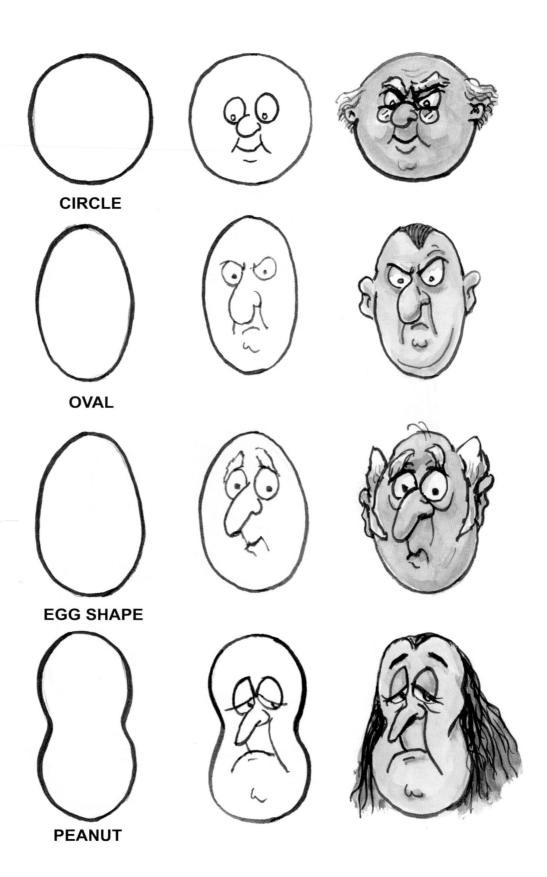

CIRCLE

OVAL

EGG SHAPE

PEANUT

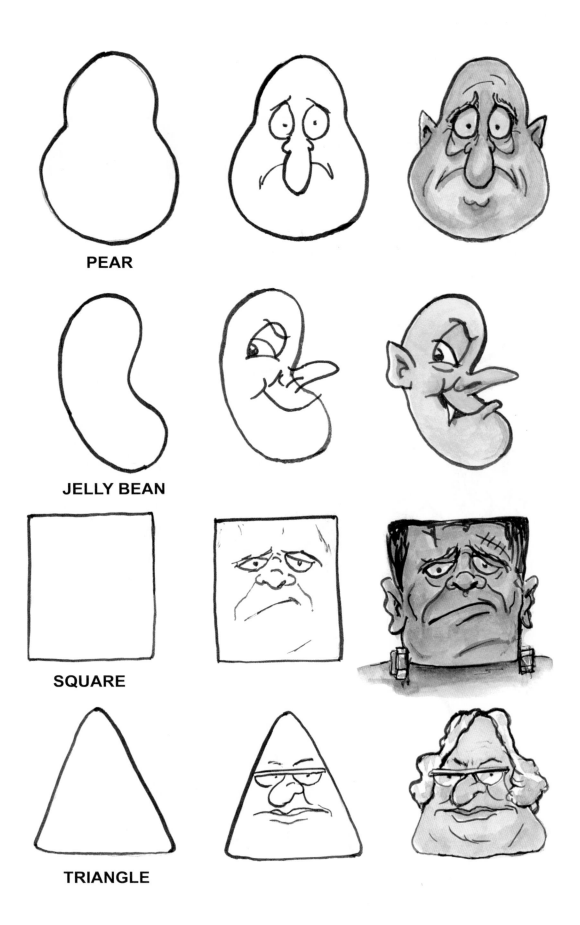

PEAR

JELLY BEAN

SQUARE

TRIANGLE

MONSTERS GALORE!

Here are more spooky heads created from simple shapes.
Now try your own!

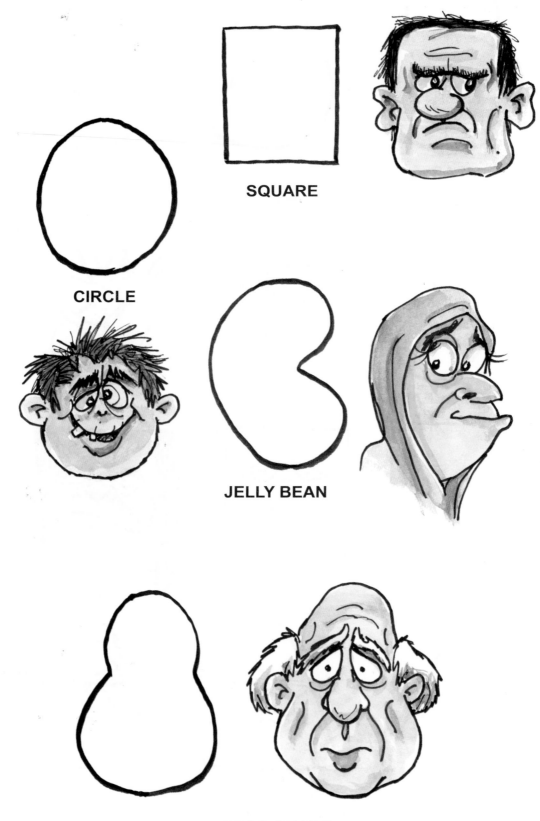

CIRCLE

SQUARE

JELLY BEAN

PEAR SHAPE

Fitting Heads to Bodies

Below are two examples of how a triangle, normal view and inverted view, can be used to portray two very different characters. This spook and skeleton seem to be enjoying their time in the cemetery!

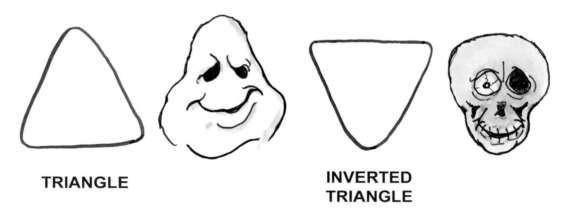

TRIANGLE

INVERTED TRIANGLE

Making Characters Younger and Older

By moving the horizontal line lower, as indicated below, you can create the appearance of a younger face.

To make the face older, reverse the process by moving the horizontal line upwards.

Note I've used an oval shape for the old man.

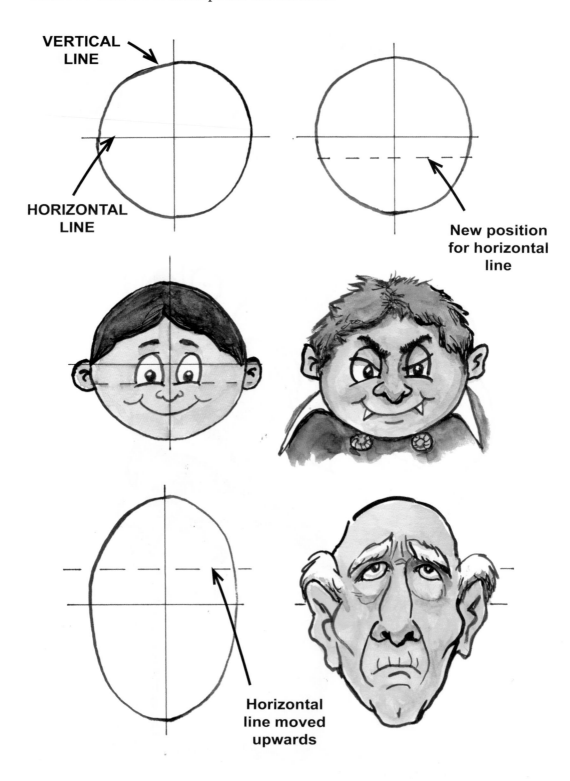

VERTICAL LINE

HORIZONTAL LINE

New position for horizontal line

Horizontal line moved upwards

Oval Head Development

Below you can see the simple development of an oval into a face. Also shown are ovals set at different angles, which here have developed into a witch's head, and a broad-faced little imp.

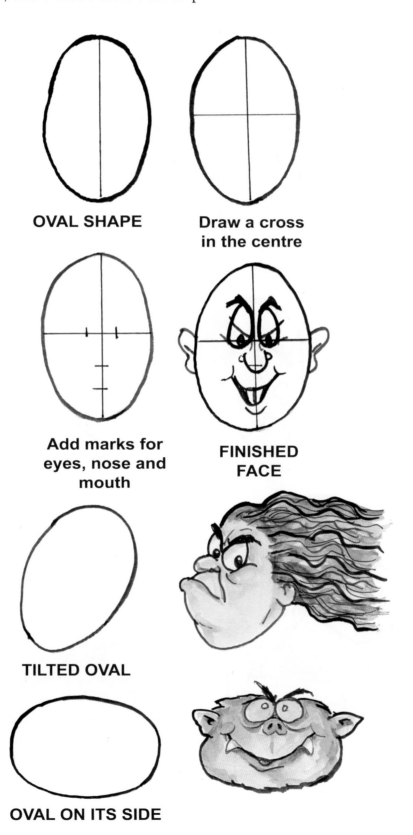

OVAL SHAPE

Draw a cross in the centre

Add marks for eyes, nose and mouth

FINISHED FACE

TILTED OVAL

OVAL ON ITS SIDE

Three-Quarter Angle

When drawing your cartoon character, decide what shaped head you want: circle, oval and so on. It is then up to you to choose the face angle. The three-quarter view is a popular angle, but is a bit trickier than the full face. The guidelines below simplify the process.

Note how the vertical line moves

Note how the vertical line moves

More Head Angles

Here are four faces made from oval shapes, using the guidelines I have shown you on the last few pages. See the final coloured images on the next page.

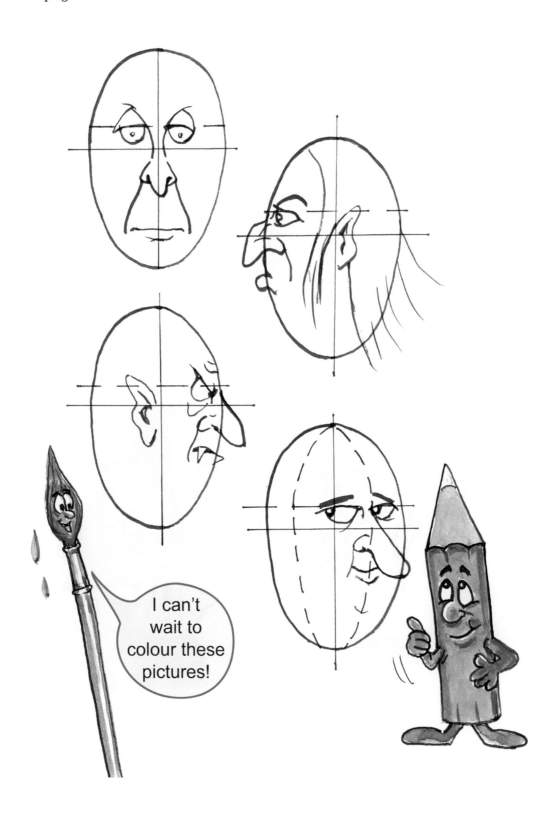

I can't wait to colour these pictures!

Below are the finished images from their development on the previous page.

Here are some examples of a ghoul, a sly manservant, a bald vampire, and a defiant witch.

Witch Business for Halloween

Let's tackle this creative witch, who has just carved a grinning face on a pumpkin.

Draw an oval as shown. This time draw two horizontal lines and move the central vertical line over to the right. This helps you to find the correct placement of the ear.

Eyes, Noses and Mouths

In order to achieve an effective cartoon face, the eyes, nose and mouth need to show a lot of expression. Yes, even the nose can have personality! See below a range of faces that will help to add character to your own cartoon faces.

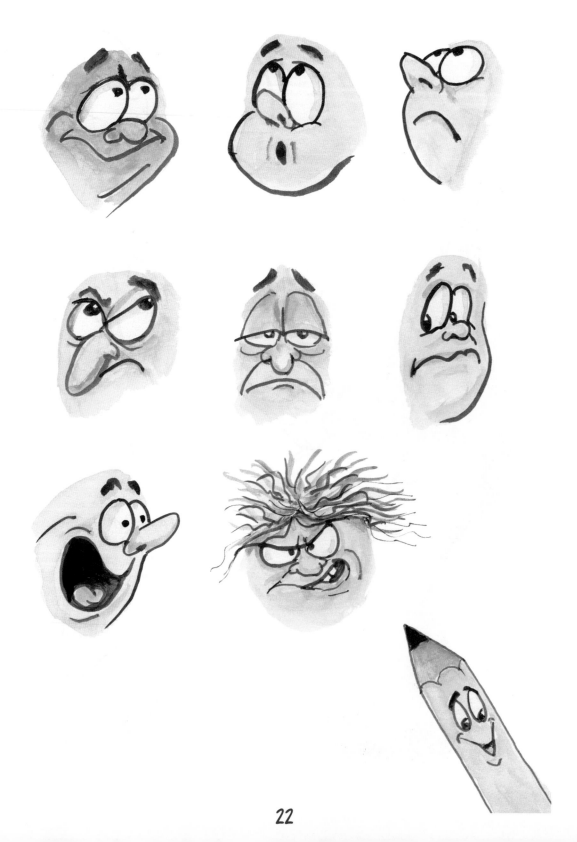

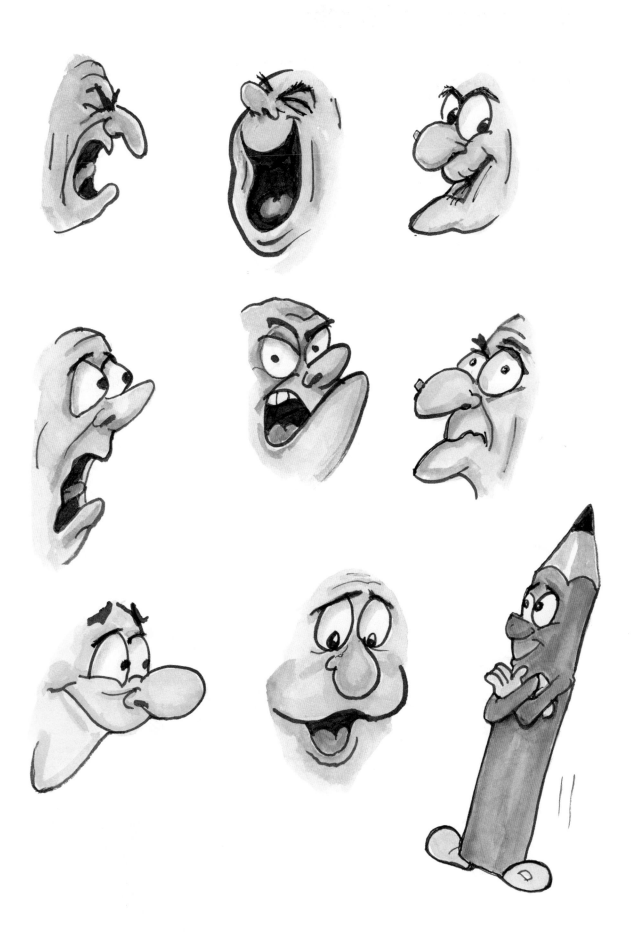

Creating Characters' Expressions

Below are a pair of ovals set at opposite angles. See how they are developed into creepy-looking individuals.

Sinister Characters

The first two images below are the coloured drawings from the step-by-step guidelines on the previous page. The rest are a display of sinister characters for you to try.

Realistic and Cartoon Hands

Compare and contrast realistic hands with cartoon hands. There is a lot less definition in cartoon hands, and in general they only have three fingers, not four.

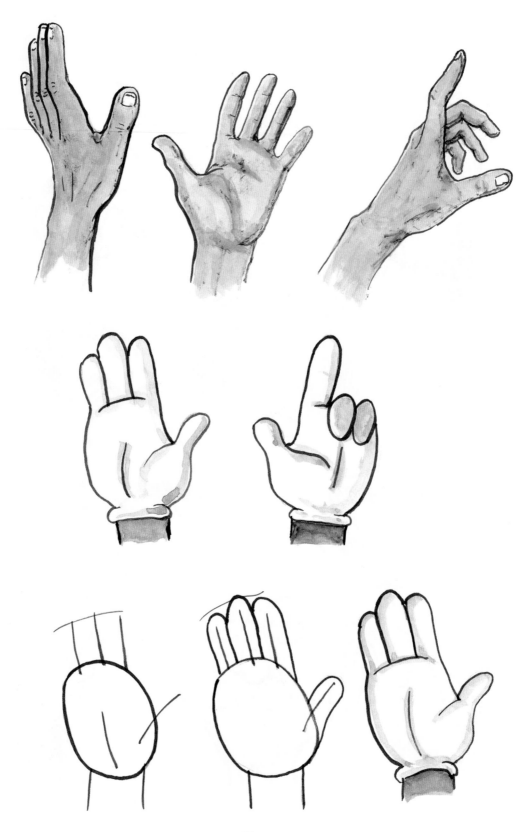

From Realistic to Cartoon Hands

Here I show you how realistic hands can be changed into cartoon hands. Some cartoon hands are midway between realism and cartoon, like the red taloned hand below which has four fingers instead of the usual three.

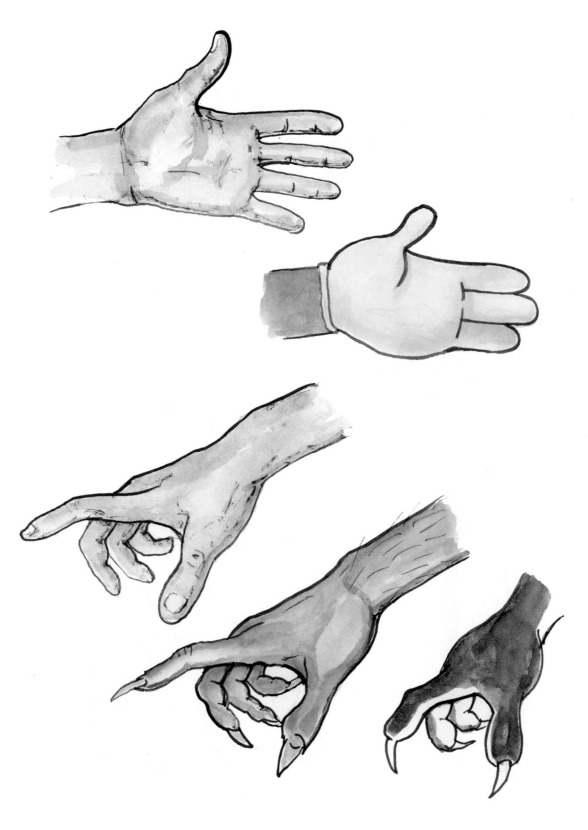

Various Hands!

Here you can see a range of different types of hands, from simple cartoon hands to sinister ones. Have fun trying to match them with different bodies!

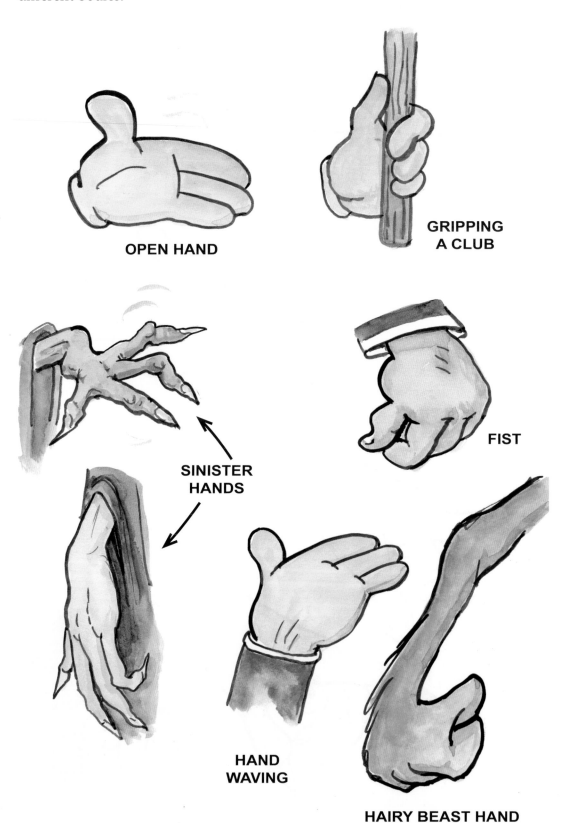

OPEN HAND

GRIPPING A CLUB

SINISTER HANDS

FIST

HAND WAVING

HAIRY BEAST HAND

Moving your Character

You can create action figures for your monster character by using the simple shapes below. First draw your desired action figure and then build up the body shape, adding clothes and other features. See pages 31 and 32 for finished examples.

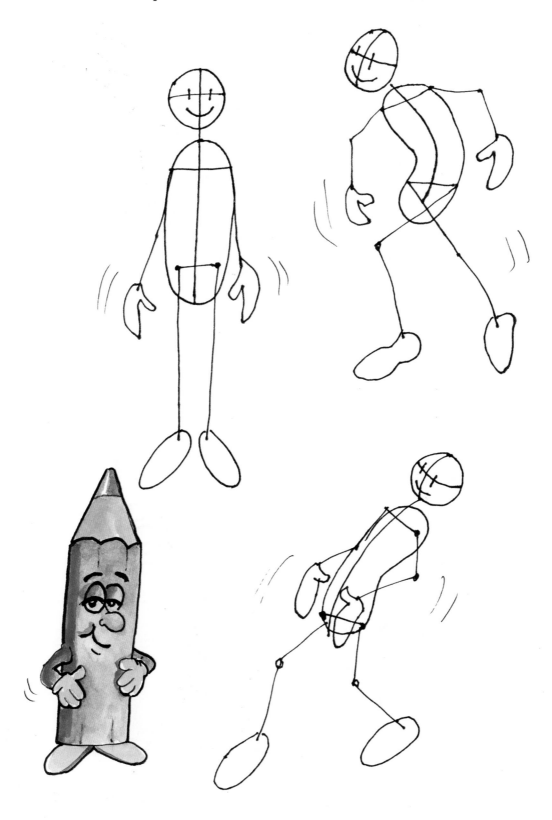

From Action Figure to Egyptian Mummy

Here is an action figure which I have developed into an animated mummy. See how I have kept the correct angles and movement of the original simple drawing in the final picture.

Check out another example on the next page.

LITTLE NOTE... Go to page 92 to see more mummys for you to draw.

From Action Figure to Quizzical Wizard

Like the example on the previous page, here is an action figure whose movement and angles have developed into a wizard. This fun character is walking along and trying to remember magic formulas.

LITTLE NOTE...
Go to pages 93 and 94 to see more wizards for you to draw.

SPOOKS AND SPIRITS

Ghostly Scream

Here is a poor pyjama-clad man running from a very scary ghost.

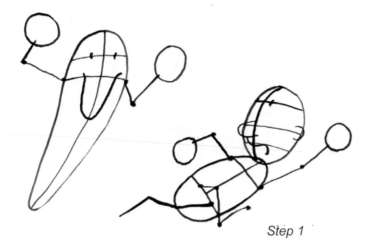

Step 1

drawing guidelines

Step 1 Draw circles and ovals to indicate body and head of man and ghost. Then add lines to indicate where facial features, arms and legs will go.

Step 2 Develop the body forms, taking care to show action and movement.

Step 3 Add more detail and rub out any unnecessary lines.

Step 2

Step 3

Step 4 Watercolour washes have been added to finish the picture. Note how the ghost can be seen better by adding a black background around it.

Doubly scary!

Now try to tackle these two malevolent ghosts – one with claw-like hands and hood, and the other a more classic creature with white hands and face.

Old Lady Spirit

This old departed spirit lady still thinks she has to walk when she could just float like a breeze!

drawing guidelines

Steps 1-4 Draw an action figure and simple shapes to show body and clothes outlines. Develop details, including the lady's hairdo and her boots! Finally add washes, giving a lighter wash to her 'spirit' form!

Step 1

Step 2

Step 3

Step 4

Young Lady Spirit

This departed spirit doesn't need to scare anyone – she is happy enough to gently float around the sky in her ethereal body.

drawing guidelines
Step 1 Draw a simple action figure and add outline shapes for hair and body.
Step 2 Build up the form and facial expression.

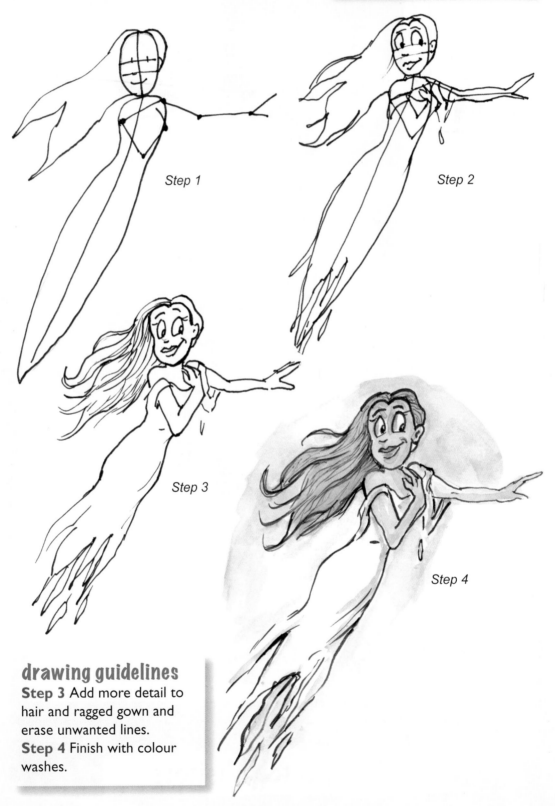

Step 1

Step 2

Step 3

Step 4

drawing guidelines
Step 3 Add more detail to hair and ragged gown and erase unwanted lines.
Step 4 Finish with colour washes.

Ghost Gallery

These ghosts just want to have fun! Have a go at drawing these simple shapes, adding different expressions and hand gestures.

High Spirits

Three cheery ghosts want to join the party. By drawing long cone shapes for Spooks 1 and 3, a pear shape for Spook 2, and by adding simple faces and arms you can create these good-natured ghosts.

WITCHES

Let's Draw Witches!

Imagine a witch and we usually think of a thin hag-like creature with a pointed hat and broom. Yet if we look at cartoons and comic books we see they come in all shapes and sizes.

I have created a series of fun books about witches and you can see the main characters featured here. They are called Abbiewail, Scarea and Grimly and are all very different personalities! Our first witch to draw is Abbiewail.

Abbiewail and the New Broom

Abbiewail's new broom seems to have a mind of its own!

drawing guidelines
Step 1 Draw an action figure and then draw circles and ovals for hands, head and body shape.
Step 2 Develop the dress outline, hair and hat. Also work on the facial expression.

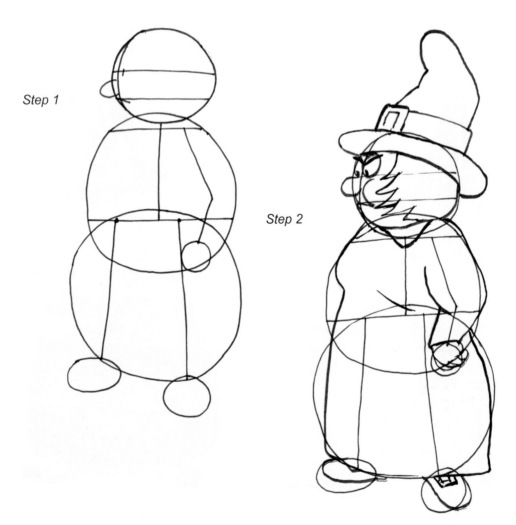

Step 1

Step 2

guidelines for broom

Step A Draw a straight line. Then add an oval shape and the beginning of twig shapes at the end.

Step B Draw two lines on either side of the line to make the pole, and develop jagged ends to the oval. Also add speed lines to show the broom's movement.

Step C (below) Finally, add colour washes to finish the image. Don't forget the L-plate on the broom!

Step 3 Add more detail and erase any unwanted lines.
Step 4 Finish your drawing by applying watercolour washes.

Step A

Step B

Step 3

Step C

Step 4

The Many Faces of Abbiewail

See if you can tackle Abbiewail's faces below, and then create your own witchy faces.

SAD

ANGRY

SHOCKED

SUSPICIOUS

NOT AMUSED

CAUTIOUS

Glamorous Scarea

Scarea is a very attractive witch. Let's follow the steps to draw her head and shoulders.

Step 1

Step 2

Step 3

Step 4

drawing guidelines

Step 1 Draw simple shapes to indicate body, head and facial features.

Step 2 Add hat, hair and develop face.

Step 3 Insert more detail and rub out any unwanted lines.

Step 4 Finish with colour washes, not forgetting the red band and border on the hat!

Grimly in a Tizzy

Grimly is the eldest of the three witch sisters and the most anxious –
always worried in case magic tricks go wrong.

drawing guidelines

Step 1 Draw an action figure and simple
shapes to create the basic structure.
Step 2 Develop features and form, also
adding Grimly's hat, wand and shoes.

Step 1

Step 2

Step 3 Add more detail. When satisfied with shape and form go over pencil lines with brush and ink. When dry erase unnecessary lines.

Step 4 Finish with colour washes. It is a good idea to make the books very different colours so that Grimly's outfit stands out more.

Step 3

Step 4

Creating a Witch's Face

See how you can create a witch's face, starting from the eyes and working outwards.

Is that supposed to be me?

Various Witches' Faces and Expressions

As I mentioned earlier, witches can have many different faces. Check out the versions below and then have a go at drawing them.

REMINDER
Go to *Getting Started* on page 9 to see how spooky faces are created.

CAUTIOUS

SUSPICIOUS

RESIGNED

NOSTALGIC

MAD

PARTY
WITCH

DAYDREAMING
WITCH

BULLY
WITCH

WITCH
IN DISGUISE

VAMPIRES

Welcome to the World of Vampires

Bram Stoker, the Irish writer who wrote the book, *Dracula*, claimed that the ghost stories his mother told him when he was a child gave him a fertile imagination. *Dracula* has spawned many a vampire tale in books, movies and television shows. Listening to your mother takes on a whole new meaning here!

Dracula Awakens

Let's draw Dracula as he is waking up from a restful sleep in his comfy coffin!

drawing guidelines
Step 1 Draw an action figure to get the right angles and movement. Then draw the coffin – feel free to use a ruler if you wish.

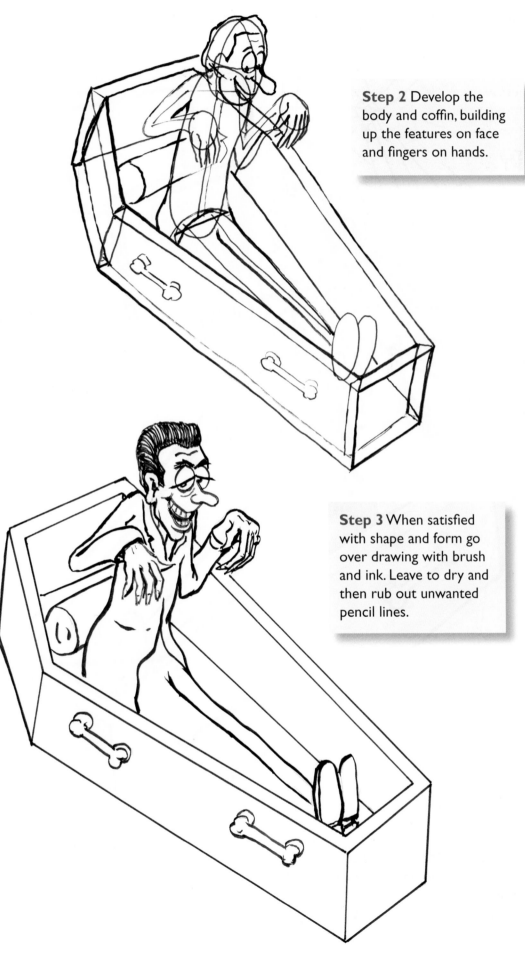

Step 2 Develop the body and coffin, building up the features on face and fingers on hands.

Step 3 When satisfied with shape and form go over drawing with brush and ink. Leave to dry and then rub out unwanted pencil lines.

Step 4 Continue to add details, adding the cobweb, scared mouse and wall. Finally, paint washes to complete your picture.

Nosferatu the Undead

Nosferatu is the German version of Dracula, imagined and made into a film in Germany back in 1920. As you can see this vampire looks a lot different from the Transylvanian Dracula!

drawing guidelines

Step 1 Draw a simple body structure.
Step 2 Start working on the taloned hands and develop the face. Also add the outline of his outfit.
Step 3 Rub out unnecessary lines and finish with watercolour washes.

Step 1

Step 2

Step 3

Count and Countess Dracula

Various Vampires

Vampires come in all shapes and sizes. When they shave they use after-grave lotion!

REMINDER
Go to *Getting Started* on page 9 to see how spooky faces are created.

More Vampires to Get your Teeth into

Take note of the framed vampire. This is drawn in a graphic novel style, and is given a more realistic approach than other cartoon vampires.

PLUMP

SINISTER

IMPISH

SUAVE

EERIE

Early Screen Vampire

This lady vampire is shown in black and white, as she would have been portrayed in movies of the 1920s and 1930s. The grey tones give an atmospheric and eerie feel to the picture . . .

Vampire Ladies

Below are a few very different female vampires: one old, one young and one a distantly elegant woman. Have a go at drawing these great characters.

HAG VAMPIRE

ELEGANT MEDIEVAL VAMPIRE

GHOSTLY GIRL VAMPIRE

GRAVE ROBBERS

Grave Concern - a Medieval Grave Robber

This despicable character is on the run after a grave robbery. It seems he has succeeded in getting away with the buried stash!

drawing guidelines

Step 1 Draw an action figure to get the right angles and movement.

Step 2 Develop the facial features, clothes and shoes. Don't forget the sacks of stolen goods!

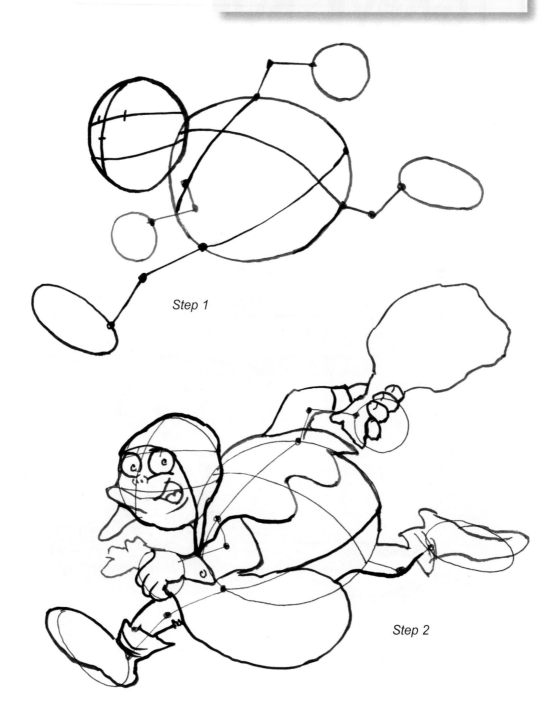

Step 1

Step 2

Step 3 Go over the pencil lines with a brush and ink. When dry, rub out unwanted pencil lines.
Step 4 Now you can enjoy adding colour washes to the finished image.

Step 3

Step 4

Victorian Grave Robber

Just as unsavoury as the previous individual, this character has only started digging into a grave. He looks confident, but there's no knowing if he will be rudely interrupted by the coppers – or a resident ghost!

Step 1

drawing guidelines

Step 1 Draw an action figure to get the right angles and movement.
Step 2 Build up the body shape and then develop the outlines of the clothes. Also take care with the top hat and the spade.

Step 2

Step 3 When happy with shapes and forms, go over pencil lines with brush and ink. When dry, rub out any unwanted pencil lines.

Step 4 Finish your drawing by adding colour washes.

Step 3

Step 4

Bony Fiddler

WEREWOLVES & ZOMBIES

Zombies on the Prowl

Always guaranteed to give good scares, zombies are shown here in their typical wide-eyed and vacant movements.

To draw them, either copy or trace action figures over these drawings and then develop the body shapes.

The framed zombie below is a graphic novel representation, portrayed more realistically than the cartoon versions.

REMINDER
Go to pages 29 and 30 to see how an action figure is created.

Werewolves on the Howl

It's no laughing matter when there's a full moon for that's the time some people turn into werewolves. Here are a few examples.

GRINNING WEREWOLF

GRUMPY WEREWOLF

SCARY WEREWOLF
(Graphic Novel Style)

HAIRY BIKER WEREWOLF

CREEPY HUMANS

Mr Hyde

Dr Jekyll has transformed into the frightening Mr Hyde. Here he is trying to avoid being noticed by people on the foggy streets of Victorian London.

drawing guidelines

Steps 1-4 Build up the simple shapes, taking care with the top hat and face expression. Then finish with sombre colour washes.

Step 1

Step 2

Step 3

Step 4

Sinister Butler

Maybe he is just leading the way to the banquet in the dining room, or maybe he has ulterior motives? We'll never know . . .

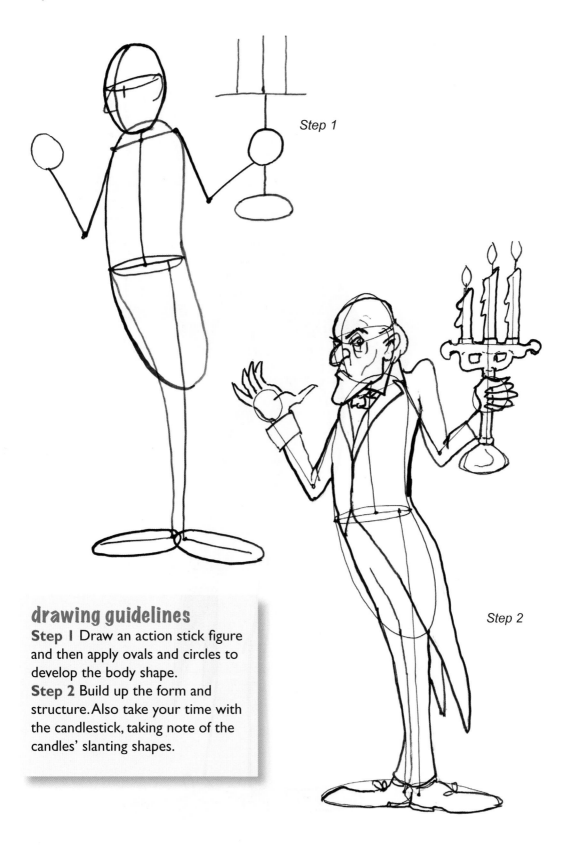

Step 1

Step 2

drawing guidelines

Step 1 Draw an action stick figure and then apply ovals and circles to develop the body shape.

Step 2 Build up the form and structure. Also take your time with the candlestick, taking note of the candles' slanting shapes.

Step 3 Rub out any unnecessary lines and add colour washes to complete your picture.

SPOOKY
FACES

The Scared, the Bad and the Ugly

Here is a fine selection of scary characters for you to enjoy drawing.

You may notice a couple of scared people have found themselves trapped in the same pages as these individuals. Cripes!

REMINDER
Go to *Getting Started*
on page 9 to see how
spooky heads are
created.

Hairy Monster on the Run

This fun-loving monster is doing his best to be scary. Has he succeeded?

drawing guidelines

Step 1 Apply ovals and circles and adjoining lines to develop the body shape.

Step 2 Build up the form and structure. Take your time to add little strokes to indicate fur.

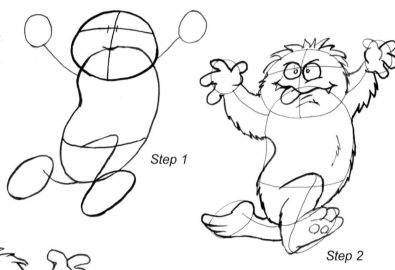

Step 1

Step 2

Step 3

Step 3 Add more details and rub out any unnecessary lines.

Step 4 Complete your drawing by painting in colourful washes.

Step 4

A Monster Selection

Here are a variety of fantastic creatures for you to tackle.

Night Mare

You wouldn't like to meet this weird horse monster on a dark night!

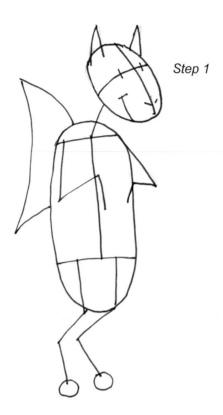

Step 1

Step 2

drawing guidelines

Steps 1-4 Build up the simple shapes, taking care with the hooves and face expression. Then finish with bright colour washes.

Step 3

Step 4

Grumpy Bigfoot

drawing guidelines

Step 1 With a pencil begin with the head. The body is like a large egg. Indicate where the arm and legs will go.

Step 2 Work up shape and features. When satisfied, go over finished drawing with brush and ink. Rub out unwanted pencil lines.

Step 3 Colour in Bigfoot as shown.

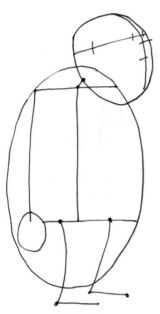

Step 1

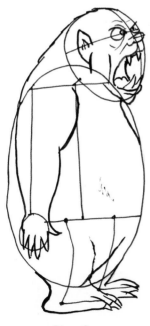

Step 2

Step 3

A Big Monster Hello

GIANTS AND OGRES

Gentle Giant

This giant just wants to be friends with humans! But whenever he approaches people they just run away . . .

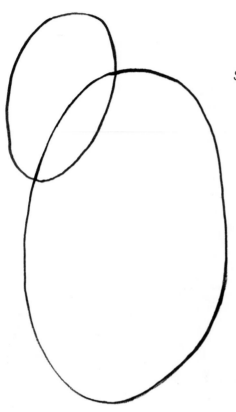

Step 1

drawing guidelines

Step 1 Draw two ovals to indicate body and head.

Step 2 See how an action figure added to these ovals develops the structure. Also note how the head is positioned lower than normal to show a hunched figure.

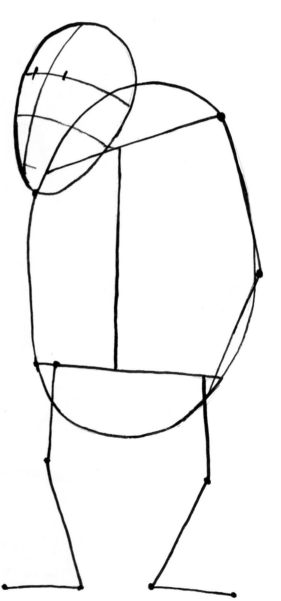

Step 2

Step 3

Step 3 Build up the details of clothes and facial features. When satisfied with the drawing, go over pencil lines with brush and ink.

Step 4 Rub out unwanted lines and colour in to finish your picture of the giant.

Step 4

Obnoxious Ogres

You wouldn't want to get on the wrong side of these ogres. They are only too willing to start a fight . . .

Headless Man and Marley's Ghost

This headless aristocrat seems rather surprised his head is not attached to his body, whereas poor Marley's ghost looks as if he has seen one too many frights!

Jinn and Genie

The word 'Genie' is derived from the Arabic word 'Jinn' or 'Djinn'.
Jinns and Genies are known as fiery creatures, similar to the demons in
Western culture. They inhabit lonely desolate places such as deserts or deep
underground caves, or even the sky.
Most are considered enemies of humans, yet not all are considered bad in
Middle Eastern traditions.
Some have even been tricked by sorcerers to enter into a lamp or bottle where
they have been trapped. Then wishes are demanded of them, to secure their
release.

Menacing Mummys

Unlike Marley's ghost on page 90, these bandaged individuals are ready to terrify anyone who dares to approach.

Start drawing these creatures by creating action figures (see pages 29-32), and then adding form and structure. Be prepared to draw lots of lines to portray bandages!

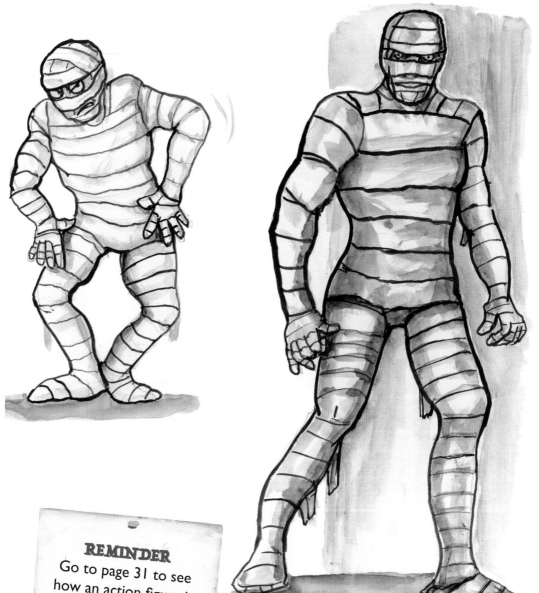

REMINDER
Go to page 31 to see how an action figure is developed into a mummy.

The mummy above has been portrayed in a more serious graphic novel style, unlike the cartoon mummy at left!

WIZARDS AND SORCERERS

Wise Wizards and Sly Sorcerers

They're all here – the good, the bad, the benevolent, the studious – even a lizard wizard. Use the techniques learned in this book to create your own unique magic-maker.

REMINDER
Go to page 32 to see how an action figure is developed into a wizard.

FIVE NEW DRAWING BOOKS
by
DON CONROY

Now that you have read *Draw with Don Monsters Galore!*, why not try more in this exciting range of easy-to-follow, educational and fun drawing books?

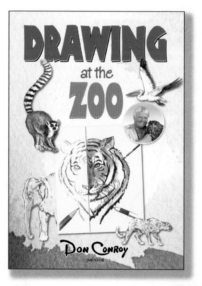

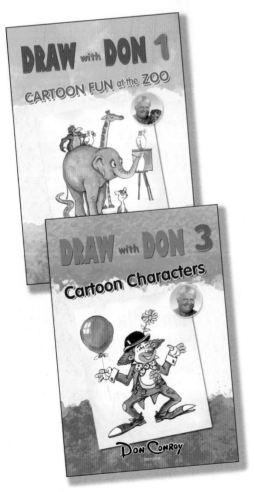